30 Days Ablaze

30 Days Ablaze

Daily Devotionals to Help You Grow Closer to God

VINCE LAMBERT

Foreword by Phil Schneider

Published by Greatness Makers
PO Box 213067, Columbia, SC 29221

www.GreatnessMakers.com

LCCN: 2023917601
ISBN: 979-8-9879354-6-0 (paperback)
ISBN: 979-8-9879354-7-7 (eBook)

Available in paperback and eBook

Dedication

This book is dedicated to my amazing partner and wife of the last 28 years, LaTonia. I am so blessed to share my life with her. She has a unique balance of beauty, kindness, and spiritual maturity. This book would not have come to pass without her constant encouragement. I am blessed daily by her humor, grace, tenacity, companionship, and wise counsel. She is a wonderful mother to my sons, and she is all I could have ever asked for in a wife. She had great influence on the completion of this book, and I celebrate her and all that God is doing through her.

Contents

Foreword

Thirty-two years ago, I bought a house that I never intended to own. I let it sit fallow for a year before I began the 3-month rehab. That project birthed a new and lifetime hobby of flipping houses. Every week, I used my day off to paint, clean, and re-envision the finished work. There's something powerful about repairing pipes that have been clogged over time, patching holes in the drywall that were opened by anger and installing hardwood where filthy carpets once laid. It is amazing that people can grow use to living in the middle of brokenness. Dealing with the areas that are fractured and using the tools designed for the job makes the work enjoyable and profitable.

So it is with our lives! Our Father has given us the tools to take the old, broken areas of our lives and renew and revitalize us. His desire is to make us into a dwelling place for His Spirit. He gives us what it takes to renew our minds, helping us to live out His best plan for our lives. The tools of prayer and the tool of scripture reshape our lives through the master craftsmanship of our Heavenly Father. We begin to see the marvelous results of His handiwork in our lives as the old areas are renewed in God's vision and plan for your life. I encourage you to use this wonderful devotional by Vince Lambert to light your fire and stoke your passion to be what God has designed you to be! Let the

Lord use Vince to point you to the path, stepping out of brokenness and into the provision and plan of God for your life!

> Phil Schneider
> District Superintendent
> Illinois Assemblies of God

Epigraph

HEBREWS 4:12

For the word of God is alive and powerful. It is sharper than the sharpest two-edged sword, cutting between soul and spirit, between joint and marrow. It exposes our innermost thoughts and desires.

***

Trust God with Every Outcome
DAY 1

Then Nebuchadnezzar flew into a rage and ordered that Shadrach, Meshach, and Abednego be brought before him. When they were brought in, Nebuchadnezzar said to them, "Is it true, Shadrach, Meshach, and Abednego, that you refuse to serve my gods or to worship the gold statue I have set up? I will give you one more chance to bow down and worship the statue I have made when you hear the sound of the musical instruments. But if you refuse, you will be thrown immediately into the blazing furnace. And then what god will be able to rescue you from my power?" Shadrach, Meshach, and Abednego replied, "O Nebuchadnezzar, we do not need to defend ourselves before you. If we are thrown into the blazing furnace, the God whom we serve is able to save us. He will rescue us from your power, Your Majesty. But even if he doesn't, we want to make it clear to you,

Your Majesty, that we will never serve your gods or worship the gold statue you have set up."

Daniel 3:13-18

The three Hebrew boys refused to compromise what they knew to be the will of God. In the midst of danger, they stood firm in their faith. Believers today have different ways we can compromise our faith to fit into the culture. These young men serve as an example of how we are to trust God in challenging moments. Though the outcome looked deadly, they still trusted God. We are called to live by faith, not by what we see. When situations look dire, our belief in God allows us to trust him with every outcome, knowing he will make a way. When we trust God in these kinds of moments, it allows him an avenue to do the miraculous. When God does the miraculous, his name is glorified. We should seek every opportunity to be vessels of the Lord that point to him and glorify him.

Prayer - Lord, great is your faithfulness! Help me to trust you with every moment of my life and in every situation, regardless of how challenging it may seem.

To ponder: What difficult situation is tempting you to compromise your faith today? How can you remain faithful to the will of God?

Stir Today's Flame

We Have All We Need
DAY 2

By his divine power, God has given us everything we need for living a godly life. We have received all of this by coming to know him, the one who called us to himself by means of his marvelous glory and excellence. And because of his glory and excellence, he has given us great and precious promises. These are the promises that enable you to share his divine nature and escape the world's corruption caused by human desires.

2 Peter 1:3-4

God has given us all we need to walk in our purpose and live the Godly life he intends for us to live. We already have it, we just need to remember what we do and who we are. We are lacking nothing. Many fall for the deception that they are lacking something. This causes us to chase things that may not be healthy for us. It prevents us from living in contentment and clouds our focus.

When we remember that God has already given us all we need, it allows us to flow in what he wants us to do, and we live in contentment, peace, and joy because we are not constantly trying to fill an imaginary void.

We receive all of this by knowing God intimately and personally. The more we know him, the more we increase in grace and peace and the more we want to know him. We have also been given great and precious promises and these promises help us to share in his nature, meaning we become like Jesus Christ.

We are conformed to his image, and because of his promises we have been given what we need to overcome every fleshly desire and temptation. It is the power of God living in us that helps us to overcome!

Prayer - Lord, help me to remember that I have everything I need to do all that you have called me to, and that I am lacking nothing!

To ponder: In what area of your life have you been tempted to believe you must strive rather than rest in your identity?

Stir Today's Flame

Keep the Focus on the Lord

DAY 3

But Moses pleaded with the Lord, "O Lord, I'm not very good with words. I never have been, and I'm not now even though you have spoken to me. I get tongue-tied, and my words get tangled."

Exodus 4:10

God gives Moses a large task and Moses has doubt if he can accomplish it. Moses uses the word "I" or some form of "I" or "I'm" four times in just one verse. This shows that Moses has too much attention on himself and his own abilities. When God calls us to something, we have a tendency to process the task according to what we think are our own abilities. Since God is calling us, the focus should be on HIS abilities not ours. God can accomplish and do whatever he wants, he is just looking for willing vessels who will not allow self-doubt to prevent them from moving forward into what God has for them.

Prayer- Lord help me keep my focus on you and YOUR abilities. Help me to live a life of obedience regardless of the size of the task.

To ponder: What is God asking of you that is so large that it requires you to keep your focus on him and what he can do?

Stir Today's Flame

Be Fruitful
DAY 4

"I am the true grapevine, and my Father is the garden-
er. He cuts off every branch of mine that doesn't produce
fruit, and he prunes the branches that do bear fruit so
they will produce even more."

John 15:1-2

Jesus says the Father cuts off every branch that does not bear fruit. This emphatically illustrates that bearing fruit is the will of God for his children. The Lord intends for his people to bear fruit in whatever we are doing for him. We cannot afford to become distracted from our purpose, or from the bearing of fruit. God loves to use us and to send us forth. When we begin to bear fruit, the Lord prunes or trims and adjusts things so that we can bear even more fruit. This is why we must be flexible in the Master's hand and allow him to trim and prune where necessary to cause further growth. This can apply to current situations, assignments, or relationships. God can be trusted with our lives, and we must submit to what HE wants to do through us.

Prayer: Lord, help me to be fruitful today.

To ponder: What are the most fruitful areas of your life? Are there any areas that are not bearing the fruit that God intends?

Stir Today's Flame

_____

_____

_____

_____

_____

_____

_____

_____

_____

_____

_____

_____

_____

_____

_____

_____

_____

_____

_____

_____

_____

_____

_____

Exercise Your Gift
DAY 5

"This is what the dream means," Joseph said. "The three branches represent three days. Within three days Pharaoh will lift you up and restore you to your position as his chief cup-bearer. And please remember me and do me a favor when things go well for you. Mention me to Pharaoh, so he might let me out of this place. For I was kidnapped from my homeland, the land of the Hebrews, and now I'm here in prison, but I did nothing to deserve it."

Genesis 40:12-15

Due to a number of challenging circumstances, Joseph finds himself in jail. Even while incarcerated, he does not cease operating where he is gifted. It does not matter where you are or what context you find yourself in, we should be active in the gifts God has given. Joseph could have felt sorry for himself or gotten angry with God, but he remained faithful to God and continued to utilize his gifts. We should never allow ourselves to get down because of a challenging situation because God still intends to use us, and he still has a plan for our lives.

Lord, help me to recognize my gifts and to steward them for your glory.

To ponder: Are you familiar with what your gifts are? If so, are you exercising them in the way that glorifies God? If you are not familiar with your gifts, what steps can you take to become more familiar with what they are?

Stir Today's Flame

Control Your Impulses
DAY 6

The man said, "Who made you ruler and judge over us? Are you thinking of killing me as you killed the Egyptian?" Then Moses was afraid and thought, "What I did must have become known."

Exodus 2:14 NIV

M oses killed a man out of impulse. This one act caused him to have to leave town. Moses shows that acting on impulse can put us in an uncomfortable situation. If we are going to be all that God intends for us to be, we must control our impulses. Acting on impulse prevents us from asking God what we should do in a given moment, and puts our flesh in the driver's seat. Before we act, we should ask God what HE wants us to do rather than taking matters into our own hands. Many believers have postponed or derailed what God had planned for them because they could not rein in their impulses. Not acting in anger or any other impulse demonstrates the character of God.

Prayer: Lord, help me to reflect your glory by keeping my impulses under your authority.

To ponder: When are you most challenged in controlling your impulses? What kinds of situations tempt you more than others? Ask the Holy Spirit to assist you in this area.

Stir Today's Flame

Holy in Every Way
DAY 7

Now may the God of peace make you holy in every way and may your whole spirit and soul and body be kept blameless until our Lord Jesus Christ comes again. God will make this happen, for he who calls you is faithful.
1 Thessalonians 5:23-24

God is continually working in us to make us holy in every way. In our thought life, in our actions, in our words, and in our perspective. There may be areas of our lives that God is still maturing and growing, and by the Spirit HE makes us holy. By the Spirit's work, we are sanctified and made into the image of Christ. We can rest in that fact because God is faithful. So even if we stumble, the work the Lord is doing in us continues.

Prayer: Lord, I bring every area of my life before you and I ask that you will cleanse and sanctify every area of my life.

To ponder: In what ways have you noticed that God's sanctification is taking place in your life? Is there any way that you have resisted the Lord's transformation?

Stir Today's Flame

Where Is Your Focus?
DAY 8

So we don't look at the troubles we can see now; rather, we fix our gaze on things that cannot be seen. For the things we see now will soon be gone, but the things we cannot see will last forever.

2 Corinthians 4:18

P aul does not say that believers will never have challenges, he just advises us to not focus on them. Troubles may exist but we must be mindful of our focus. Instead of focusing on our troubles, he says to gaze on what can't be seen. God is active even when it is not obvious or easily visible. We must keep our focus on eternal things. If we only gaze at what we can physically see, we can be deceived into believing the lie that God is not doing anything and nothing is breaking your way. If we keep an eternal view and perspective, we will never doubt God's hand on us. After all, what we can see now in the natural is only temporary, but the things that God is doing in the Spirit realm are eternal. When the natural overshadows the Spiritual, the natural has too much of our focus.

Prayer: Lord, help me to remember that my relationship with you is eternal. Allow me to stay focused on the things that glorify you so I will not be distracted by the things in the world.

To ponder: Where has your gaze been fixed most recently? Has it been on the things of the world or on the things of God? Going forward, how can you ensure your focus stays in the right place?

Stir Today's Flame

Mercy
DAY 9

When God our Savior revealed his kindness and love, he saved us, not because of the righteous things we had done, but because of his mercy. He washed away our sins, giving us a new birth and new life through the Holy Spirit.

Titus 3:4-5

We have been given mercy, and our lives have been cleansed. Because of the cross, we have been given a new life in Christ. These mercies are new every day. We live this new life under the power of the Holy Spirit. We do not toil in works, but we live in God's Spirit. The Holy Spirit gives us the power to resist sin and to walk in holiness and God's wisdom. We must embrace the new position we have been given and walk in the freedom we have been granted.

Prayer: Lord, thank you for the mercy you have shown me today and every day. Help me show others the same kind of mercy you have granted me.

To ponder: In what specific way has the Lord shown you mercy? How can you duplicate that mercy to others?

Stir Today's Flame

Blessed to Be a Blessing
DAY 10

I appeal to you to show kindness to my child, Onesimus.
I became his father in the faith while here in prison.
Onesimus hasn't been of much use to you in the past, but
now he is very useful to both of us. I am sending him
back to you, and with him comes my own heart.

Philemon 1:10-12

P aul makes an appeal on behalf of Onesimus. He supports him
and utilizes his influence on another's behalf. Many times, God
gives us influence to come to the aid of someone else. We should utilize
the relationships that we have to further the gospel and to assist others
when we can. Paul was assisted in a similar way by Barnabas, who
helped Paul to develop relationships with the other Apostles at the
beginning of his ministry. Here he does the same for Onesimus. We
should look to open doors for others as this demonstrates the heart of
God.

Prayer: Give me a heart to bless others.

To ponder: Who in your life can you show special favor to today?

Stir Today's Flame

Endure Through Testing
DAY 11

Since he himself has gone through suffering and testing,
he is able to help us when we are being tested.

Hebrews 2:18

J esus was tested beyond anything that we could ever experience. Through his testing and suffering, he endured and was victorious. It is because of his victory that we also have the ability to get victory. Even when we are tested, victory is available. It is up to us to walk in the victory that Jesus made available on the cross. It all comes down to being aware of God's presence at all times and calling on him when we need him.

Prayer: Lord, help me to experience victory in every area of my life.

To ponder: Is there an area in your life where you're not experiencing victory in Christ? If so, how can you ensure victory in that area?

Stir Today's Flame

Resist
DAY 12

Do not let sin control the way you live; do not give in to sinful desires.

Romans 6:12

Paul uses the key term "let" here. The word means 'to allow'. This tells us that we have the ability to control what we do and how we respond to situations around us. He says do not give in, meaning that we must resist everything that is not like God. This takes being intentional and being vigilant in our daily lives. We are able to resist because of who we are in Christ. The previous verse tells us we are dead to sin. THIS is who we are, not the one who is willfully sinning. We have the authority to walk in freedom, we just have to exercise it.

Prayer: Lord help me resist anything that is not going to draw me closer to you.

To ponder: Where in your life do you need to further submit to God to resist the enemy's influence in your life?

Stir Today's Flame

Pursue Righteousness

DAY 13

Because of the weakness of your human nature, I am using the illustration of slavery to help you understand all of this. Previously, you let yourselves be slaves to impurity and lawlessness, which led ever deeper into sin. Now you must give yourselves to be slaves to righteous living so that you will become holy.

Romans 6:19

Before we came to Christ, we were slaves to sin. As a matter of fact, we allowed ourselves to sin. Then, it was our lifestyle. It took no effort and it came naturally. Now we are not slaves to sin, but we should be slaves to righteousness. We now give ourselves to righteousness, which then leads to holiness. Since it is still natural to want to do what the flesh wants, we must be intentional about pursuing righteousness. We must be fascinated with God and fascinated with his presence. The very pursuit of righteousness produces holiness and godly character.

Prayer: Thank you for allowing me to experience freedom and for making me the righteousness of God.

To ponder: How is the new life of righteousness reflected in your daily life?

Stir Today's Flame

100% Obedience
DAY 14

Jesus replied, "'You must love the Lord your God with all your heart, all your soul, and all your mind.' This is the first and greatest commandment."

Matthew 22:37-38

L oving God partially is not an option. If we are going to be God's people, then we MUST love him with everything that is in us. We cannot love and serve God halfway, but he requires a full commitment from us. This text shows what that commitment looks like. Our heart is our passion; we love God with great passion and commitment. Our soul is our will and our emotions. Our will should line up with his and we must keep our emotions subject to the Holy Spirit. We also love God with our minds. Our minds should think the thoughts of Christ and reject whatever is not from him.

Prayer: Lord, I trust you with everything in me. Help me to live in obedience completely.

To ponder: Are you loving and obeying the Lord completely in your life right now? If not, what area has the most struggle for you?

Stir Today's Flame

A Consistent Model
DAY 15

Keep putting into practice all you learned and received from me—everything you heard from me and saw me doing. Then the God of peace will be with you.

Philippians 4:9

P aul tells the Philippian church to keep or to continue putting into practice what he'd taught them. First, we must actually implement what God shows us and what we learn in his word. It is not enough just to hear the truth; we must implement it and live it. Then we must do it consistently. We must be people who live for God day in and day out. Consistency is what makes the difference. We can't half-step in our walk with God; we must be committed and focused each day. Then he says, "all that you saw me do". We must be people who are models for others. What kind of a model are you? We have to be people who are consistent models for others because you reproduce not what you present or what you want to be, but you reproduce who you are. If we live for God daily, it helps us to be consistent models for Jesus. Not inconsistent or hot and cold. If we model inconsistency, people will believe that God is inconsistent. In reality, he is anything but.

Prayer: Help me live consistently before you.

To ponder: In what areas of your life are you the most consistent and the least consistent? What adjustments can you make to reflect God's character?

Stir Today's Flame

Our Refuge and Our Strength

DAY 16

God is our refuge and strength, always ready to help in times of trouble.

Psalm 46:1

God is a refuge, which is a place of safety and strength. Meaning, he gives us the ability to overcome what is in front of us. Refuge makes us feel safe and covered, and strength helps us to feel empowered to overcome obstacles and obtain victory. God is both to us. So, when we feel pressure or difficulty, we run to him not to the things of the world. Many times, we can be tempted to find a cheap substitute, but God is the only one who will bring us true fulfillment.

Prayer: Lord, help me stay aware of the strength and protection that you have already provided.

To ponder: Where have you been tempted to substitute other things instead of resting in God being your refuge and strength?

Stir Today's Flame

Focus on the Unseen
DAY 17

So we don't look at the troubles we can see now; rather, we fix our gaze on things that cannot be seen. For the things we see now will soon be gone, but the things we cannot see will last forever.

2 Corinthians 4:18

In this life we may experience challenges, but we must live in the Spirit. We cannot expect to flow in revelation if we are living based solely on the natural world. We must tap into the Spirit. The Spirit world is even more real than the natural world. We stay focused on the things of the Spirit when we are focused on God and his word. The more we surrender ourselves to his word, the more revelation we walk in. This is why the spiritual disciplines are so important for the believer because they help us to stay tapped into the Spirit. The enemy wants us to live apart from God and solely in the natural realm, so we will be weakened and not prepared for his attacks. We must stay fortified!

Prayer: Lord, continue to grow my discipline to interact with you each and every day.

To ponder: How is your devotional life? In what specific ways can you enhance it?

Stir Today's Flame

Keep Your Eye Gate Pure
DAY 18

"Your eye is like a lamp that provides light for your body. When your eye is healthy, your whole body is filled with light. But when your eye is unhealthy, your whole body is filled with darkness. And if the light you think you have is actually darkness, how deep that darkness is!

Matthew 6:22-23

Our eyes give us access to either darkness or light. We must monitor what we allow to go into our eye gate. Things that go into our eye gate that are not healthy can stir us to sin (lust, jealousy, anxiety, fear, etc.). The good news is that we have control over what goes into our eye gate and ultimately our minds. If we fill our eyes and minds with things that agree with God and his word, we will live in righteousness and freedom but if we fill our minds with the things that will stir us to sin, death is the result.

Prayer: Lord, I thank you for giving me the ability to determine what goes into my eye gate. I pray that I only entertain those things that glorify you.

To ponder: Is there any area of compromise that you are allowing into your eye gate? What steps can you take to rectify this?

Stir Today's Flame

Stalked by the Love of God
DAY 19

Surely your goodness and unfailing love will pursue me all the days of my life, and I will live in the house of the Lord forever.

Psalm 23:6

It is an amazing truth to know the love of God is in pursuit of us at all times. There is never a time when God is not pursuing us. It lasts for our entire life. He is always seeking to connect with us. He loves us no matter what we may have experienced. On our best day, he loves and is pursuing us; on our worst day, he loves us and is pursuing us. God in his infinite mercy never runs short or is lacking in grace. The grace of God is bigger than anything we can say, do, or think. He loves us no matter what.

Prayer: Lord, thank you for your love that never runs out.

To ponder: Do you have a full understanding of God's love? How much do you really believe it?

Stir Today's Flame

Show Me Your Glory
DAY 20

The Lord replied, "I will make all my goodness pass before you, and I will call out my name, Yahweh, before you. For I will show mercy to anyone I choose, and I will show compassion to anyone I choose. But you may not look directly at my face, for no one may see me and live." The Lord continued, "Look, stand near me on this rock. As my glorious presence passes by, I will hide you in the crevice of the rock and cover you with my hand until I have passed by. Then I will remove my hand and let you see me from behind. But my face will not be seen."

Exodus 33:19-23

This is a powerful scene! The glory of the Lord was so intense that Moses could only withstand the backside of it after being hidden in the cleft of a rock and covered. This shows how powerful God's presence is! We should seek after his presence above all else. There is nothing more magnificent or fascinating than the glorious presence of God. The amazing part is that once we know Christ as savior, his presence is inside of us and never leaves us. Enjoy the presence of the Lord today!

Prayer: Lord, I thank you that your presence is with me regardless of what I may face today.

To ponder: What is a practical way that you can enjoy the Lord's presence today?

Stir Today's Flame

The Power of God at Work
DAY 21

For I am not ashamed of this Good News about Christ.
It is the power of God at work, saving everyone who
believes—the Jew first and also the Gentile.

Romans 1:16

Paul declares he is not ashamed of the gospel. He is fully embracing the gospel (good news) of Christ and all that it means. The gospel is the power of God at work. The gospel is at work in the hearts of all believers. It is at work not only leading us to salvation, but it is also at work freeing us from bondage and getting us delivered from condemnation. The power of the gospel is always working in us and on our behalf. The power of the gospel is never dormant or stagnant. It is always working, and it is working for our good and our benefit. Even when it seems like it is not at work, it is. The gospel of Jesus Christ is that powerful and can do all those things.

Prayer: Lord, may I never forget that the power of the gospel is continually at work in me.

To ponder: After coming to Christ, how have you seen the power of the gospel at work on your behalf?

Stir Today's Flame

Free from Sin's Obligation
DAY 22

*Therefore, dear brothers and sisters, you have no oblig-
ation to do what your sinful nature urges you to do. For
if you live by its dictates, you will die. But if through
the power of the Spirit you put to death the deeds of your
sinful nature, you will live. For all who are led by the
Spirit of God are children of God.*

Romans 8:12-14

Not only are we not obligated to obey our sinful nature, but
if we do obey, it is typically followed by death. We have a
choice to choose death or life. The power to choose lies within us.
We can only make godly decisions by living through the power of the
Spirit. We cannot live by the Law and its dictates, but we must receive
the life-giving power that comes from walking with Jesus. We don't
perform to persuade God to love us, but we live in obedience because
of the love we have been given. We love God and we don't want to

disappoint him because of our relationship with him through Christ, and the price that has been paid.

Prayer: Lord, thank you for giving me the ability the make decisions to glorify you. Help me to recognize the lies of the enemy and to resist by the power of your Holy Spirit.

To ponder: What areas are you yielding to the Lord? What areas have you experienced freedom and deliverance in the Lord?

Stir Today's Flame

Confession is Good for the Soul

DAY 23

If I had not confessed the sin in my heart, the Lord would not have listened. But God did listen! He paid attention to my prayer. Praise God, who did not ignore my prayer or withdraw his unfailing love from me.

Psalm 66:18-20

The confession of sin is of critical importance to the believer's relationship with God. If we do not confess our sin, it leaves unfinished business between us and God. This hinders our ability to pray and to live by faith. Unconfessed sin makes us sin-conscious and hinders our ability to be bold in Jesus. When we do confess our sin, it clears the slate and reconnects us to the living God. He wipes away the condemnation and fear so that we can walk in intimacy with him again. This is how our prayer life grows. God will not ignore our prayers when we confess our sins and look to connect with him.

He loves us more than we love ourselves. And he desires to be in connection with us.

Prayer: Lord, I confess known sin in my life. I bring it to you now openly and claim the promise of 1 John 1:9 that says you are faithful and just to forgive and cleanse me.

To ponder: Is there an area in your life that you have not openly confessed before the Lord? If so, take some time today to approach a loving and merciful God.

Stir Today's Flame

_____

_____

_____

_____

_____

_____

_____

_____

_____

_____

_____

_____

_____

_____

_____

_____

_____

_____

_____

_____

_____

_____

Overcoming Temptation
DAY 24

Then Jesus was led by the Spirit into the wilderness to be tempted there by the devil. For forty days and forty nights he fasted and became very hungry. During that time the devil came and said to him, "If you are the Son of God, tell these stones to become loaves of bread." Jesus told him, "No! The Scriptures say, 'People do not live by bread alone, but by every word that comes from the mouth of God.'" Then the devil took him to the holy city, Jerusalem, to the highest point of the Temple, and said, "If you are the Son of God, jump off! For the Scriptures say, 'He will order his angels to protect you. And they will hold you up with their hands so you won't even hurt your foot on a stone.'" Jesus responded, "The Scriptures also say, 'You must not test the Lord your God.'" Next the devil took him to the peak of a very high mountain and showed him all the kingdoms of the world and their glory. "I will give it all to you," he said, "if you will kneel down and worship me." "Get out of here, Satan," Jesus told him. "For the Scriptures say, 'You must worship the

Lord your God and serve only him.'" Then the devil
went away, and angels came and took care of Jesus.

Matthew 4:1-11

J esus was Lord, yet he was still tempted by the enemy. If Jesus
himself was tempted by Satan, we can also expect to be. Here the
enemy tempted Jesus when he was hungry. He tempted him with food
to entice him to act independent of God. Since Jesus was hungry, that
is where he was the most vulnerable. Satan can attack us when we are
most vulnerable. Jesus resisted by using the word of God. God's word
is powerful and alive. When we quote God's word as we are tempted,
worried or fearful, it strengthens us to focus our attention on God and
allows us to overcome.

Prayer: Lord, thank you for empowering me to overcome every
temptation I may face today.

To ponder: What areas of temptation are the greatest for you today?
Submit to the Holy Spirit in that area today.

Stir Today's Flame

People of the Spirit
DAY 25

For we are not fighting against flesh-and-blood enemies,
but against evil rulers and authorities of the unseen
world against mighty powers in this dark world, and
against evil spirits in the heavenly places.

Ephesians 6:12

As believers in Christ, we are in a spiritual battle. The spiritual battle we are in is not against other people, but it is against the darkness of the evil one. We must remember that no matter what things look like in the flesh, we must stay in the Spirit and not allow ourselves to operate in the flesh. There are dark spirits in the world that seek to influence us. We can keep our influence by living and staying focused on the Spirit. By keeping our attention on the Lord through prayer, Bible intake, and other spiritual disciplines, we position ourselves to be people of the Spirit.

Prayer: Lord, I thank you for helping me to realize the core root of my spiritual battles.

To ponder: What area in your life is a current spiritual battle? Know that you have been granted victory!

Stir Today's Flame

Humility
DAY 26

While they were at Hazeroth, Miriam and Aaron criticized Moses because he had married a Cushite woman. They said, "Has the Lord spoken only through Moses? Hasn't he spoken through us, too?" But the Lord heard them. (Now Moses was very humble—more humble than any other person on earth.)

Numbers 12:1-3

Miriam and Aaron were critical of Moses, but the text does not have any record of Moses responding. All it says was that Moses walked in humility. If he did respond to it directly, the Bible does not record it. It seems to emphasize his humility rather than his response. We would do well to operate in this way also. Many times, our humility is needed more than our response. Humility can defuse a situation and not allow it to escalate; humility also allows God to be God. We trust him with the outcome, and we trust him to give the right response. If we stay focused on demonstrating Christ-like character, we don't have to be overly concerned with having a right response because we trust the Lord in these situations.

Prayer: Lord, may my humility increase today.

To ponder: In what recent occurrence was your humility needed more than a verbal response?

Stir Today's Flame

Remember Your First Love
DAY 27

"But I have this complaint against you. You don't love me or each other as you did at first! Look how far you have fallen! Turn back to me and do the works you did at first. If you don't repent, I will come and remove your lampstand from its place among the churches. But this is in your favor: You hate the evil deeds of the Nicolaitans, just as I do.

Revelation 2:4-6

J esus' complaint against the church at Ephesus was that they were not doing the things they did at first, which is what created the vibrant relationship with him. It is interesting how easily God's people can sometimes get away from the things that draw us closer to him. We must make choices that will glorify God and keep us walking close to him. There are a number of things in this world that seek to come between us and God. Believers must be intentional and deliberate about choosing God and his presence.

Prayer: Help me live with the right priorities and put nothing before you, My God.

To ponder: Are you continuing to engage in the activities that will draw you closer to God, or have you allowed yourself to become laxed in your devotion to him?

Stir Today's Flame

Become a Cycle Breaker
DAY 28

But Rebekah overheard what Isaac had said to his son, Esau. So, when Esau left to hunt for the wild game, she said to her son, Jacob, "Listen. I overheard your father say to Esau, 'Bring me some wild game and prepare me a delicious meal. Then I will bless you in the Lord's presence before I die.' Now, my son, listen to me. Do exactly as I tell you. Go out to the flocks and bring me two fine young goats. I'll use them to prepare your father's favorite dish. Then take the food to your father so he can eat it and bless you before he dies."

Genesis 27:5-10

T he deception did not start with Jacob, but it was his mother Rebekah's idea. She was a deceiver before Jacob was. Jacob was that way because he saw her operate that way. What children see their parents do they will have a tendency to do, good or bad. Many of the things current generations struggle with, the seed was sown in previous generations. Each generation must decide what it will do, but the tendency certainly can be there. Each generation has to decide what cycles they want to continue and which ones they want to break. Making a decision to be the cycle breaker can have a powerful impact on the current generation and many future generations to come.

Prayer: Help me to be a breaker of any unhealthy cycles or patterns from previous generations.

To ponder: What cycles do you want to break that previous generations struggled with?

Stir Today's Flame

The Lord is with You
DAY 29

The Lord is my shepherd; I have all that I need. He lets me rest in green meadows; he leads me beside peaceful streams. He renews my strength. He guides me along right paths, bringing honor to his name. Even when I walk through the darkest valley, I will not be afraid, for you are close beside me. Your rod and your staff protect and comfort me. You prepare a feast for me in the presence of my enemies. You honor me by anointing my head with oil. My cup overflows with blessings. Surely your goodness and unfailing love will pursue me all the days of my life, and I will live in the house of the Lord forever.

Psalm 23

The 23rd Psalm is a very familiar passage, but if we are too familiar with it we can miss its power. The psalmist reminds us of who we are and who is with us. The Lord is with us no matter where we are or what situation we face. We should not allow fear to rob us of the peace that God wants us to have. We are to be people of peace, not because of us, but because of who God is. The fact that the Lord has conquered everything that needs to be conquered and that he is with us should give us all of the comfort we need. Knowing God is with us and knowing that God is for us should propel us forward into doing the will of God. The presence of God is not only with us, but is actually hunting us down! He pursues us. No matter what, the Lord is with us and is seeking connection to us. Goodness and mercy are literally stalking us so that the will of God is done in each of our lives.

Prayer: Let me never forget your presence is with me at all times.

To ponder: Have you ever felt that God was not with you? How does this Psalm prove that statement to be false?

Stir Today's Flame

_____
_____
_____
_____
_____
_____
_____
_____
_____
_____
_____
_____
_____
_____
_____
_____
_____
_____
_____
_____
_____
_____
_____
_____

Tearing Down Strongholds
DAY 30

We are human, but we don't wage war as humans do. We use God's mighty weapons, not worldly weapons, to knock down the strongholds of human reasoning and to destroy false arguments. We destroy every proud obstacle that keeps people from knowing God. We capture their rebellious thoughts and teach them to obey Christ.

2 Corinthians 10:3-5

A stronghold is a thought or reasoning that is planted in the mind of a believer. There can be strongholds that arise from current or previous life experiences. The way we battle against these strongholds is not in the flesh. We don't battle with carnal things or worldly ideas; we battle with spiritual weapons. This may seem counterintuitive to battle with a weapon that is not in the same arena as how you are being attacked, but this is the key to victory. The more worldly the attack, the more spiritual our response needs to be.

The weapon we have is our mind. We have the ability to remove and tear down the stronghold of the enemy that seeks to come against us. We can take every thought captive, but we must remember that we possess this ability. The enemy is banking on us forgetting and not knowing who we are and what we can do. God has already given us provision for the victory. The question is, are we walking in what has been provided? We must keep our minds on God to pull down strongholds. We can not allow an idle mind; it must be filled with the word and power of God.

Prayer: Help me recognize the enemies' deceptions and tear down every thought or idea that does not line up with God's word.

To ponder: Are there any current strongholds in your life? Find another trusted believer who can pray for you and walk alongside you in this area. God's will is freedom from every stronghold that would attempt to take you away from the will of God.

Stir Today's Flame

About the Author

Vince Lambert is passionate about helping believers reach their God-given potential and purpose. He has almost 30 years of experience in local church leadership in the roles of pastor, associate pastor, speaker, and church planter. He is an ordained minister and has also served for 15 years as a military Chaplain. In addition, he has served as an adjunct faculty member at several universities including, Moody Bible Institute, Trinity International University, North Park University (MBA program), Northwest University, North Central University, and Keller Graduate School of Management.

His educational background includes a BS in Finance from Chicago State University, an MBA from North Park University, a Master of Religion and Urban Ministry from Trinity Evangelical Divinity School, a Master of Human Services Counseling (Marriage & Family) from Liberty University and he is in the final stages of a Doctor of Ministry (DMin) in Pastoral Care and Counseling. He previously spent over 20 years in the business world in financial services, investments, and bank management.

Contact Vince at vincelambert.net

Want to write a book but don't know where to start?

Contact Greatness Makers Today!

Making you great is our business.

FLOWCODE

PRIVACY.FLOWCODE.COM